FEATHERED FRIENDS

HUMMINGBIRDS

Madison Parker

NORWOOD HOUSE PRESS

Library of Congress Cataloging-in-Publication Data:

Names: Parker, Madison.
Title: Hummingbirds / Madison Parker.
Description: Buffalo, NY : Norwood House Press, 2025. | Series: Feathered friends | Includes glossary and index.
Identifiers: ISBN 9781684502868 (pbk.) | ISBN 9781684502875 (library bound) | ISBN 9781684502882 (ebook)
Subjects: LCSH: Hummingbirds--Juvenile literature.
Classification: LCC QL696.A558 P375 2025 | DDC 598.7'64--dc23

Published in 2025 by
Norwood House Press
2544 Clinton Street
Buffalo, NY 14224

Designer: Ocean Books
Editor: Kim Thompson

Photo credits: Cover, pp. 1, 5, 6, 7, 14 Ondrej Prosicky/Shutterstock.com; p. 9 Chiio Segura/Shutterstock.com; p. 11 Damsea/Shutterstock.com; p. 12 Pascal De Munck/Shutterstock.com; p. 13 Ukrit.wa/Shutterstock.com; p. 16 Petr Simon/Shutterstock.com; p. 17 petrdd/Shutterstock.com; p. 18 Chelsea Sampson/Shutterstock.com; p. 19 Jodie Burkhard/Shutterstock.com; p. 21 Richard Seeley/Shutterstock.com

Printed in the United States of America

CPSIA compliance information: Batch #CW25NHP: For further information contact Norwood House Press at 1-800-237-9932.

TABLE OF CONTENTS

What Do Hummingbirds Look Like?

Hummingbirds are our feathered friends. They are tiny and colorful. They are about the size of a regular crayon.

A hummingbird's feathers **shimmer** in bright colors like green, blue, and red. Its throat often sparkles with color.

These birds have small, rounded bodies and long, narrow **beaks**. Their wings flap so fast that they look blurry.

Where Do Hummingbirds Live?

Hummingbirds live in North America and South America. They like places with lots of flowers.

They build tiny nests on tree branches. Their nests are made from plants and spiderwebs.

How Do Hummingbirds Grow Up?

Hummingbird eggs are as tiny as jelly beans. Babies **hatch** in two weeks. They fly when they are three to four weeks old.

What Do Hummingbirds Eat?

Hummingbirds love to drink **nectar** from flowers. They use their long, skinny beaks to reach deep inside the blooms.

Hummingbirds eat insects and spiders. These provide **protein** that helps them grow strong.

Hummingbirds look for food from dawn to dusk. They need to eat a lot because they move very fast. This uses up a lot of **energy**.

What Sounds Do Hummingbirds Make?

When hummingbirds fly, their wings make a humming sound. Their wings flap as quickly as 80 times each second.

Hummingbirds chirp quietly when they are near each other. It is a soft, quick sound.

When they feel **threatened**, hummingbirds make a sharp noise. It sounds like fast chattering.

They also buzz loudly when they dive through the air. This happens when they are excited or playing.

What Funny Things Can Hummingbirds Do?

Hummingbirds can fly backward and even upside down. They chase each other around like they are playing tag. They can also **hover** in one spot as if they are floating in the air!

GLOSSARY

beaks (beeks): horny, pointed jaws on birds; bird bills

energy (EN-ur-jee): the ability or strength to do something without getting tired; the ability to do work

hatch (hach): to break out of an egg to be born

hover (HUHV-ur): to hang suspended in the air; to remain in one place while in the air

nectar (NEK-tur): a sweet liquid produced by the flowering parts of plants

protein (PROH-teen): a type of chemical compound that is essential to life; meat and fish are sources of protein

shimmer (SHIM-ur): to shine with a faint, unsteady light

threatened (THRE-tuhnd): in danger of being harmed

THINKING QUESTIONS

1. What does a hummingbird look like?
2. What is special about the sounds a hummingbird makes?
3. How does a hummingbird show it is smart?
4. What do hummingbirds eat?
5. Why do you think a hummingbird is a feathered friend?

INDEX

ABOUT THE AUTHOR

Madison Parker spent her childhood in the city of Chicago, Illinois. A farm girl at heart, today she lives in Wisconsin with her husband and four children on a small farm with cows, goats, chickens, and two miniature horses named Harley and David. Her favorite dessert is vanilla frozen custard with rainbow sprinkles, even in the winter.